Technocracy: The New World Order of the Illuminati and The Battle Between Good and Evil

Dan Desmarques

Published by 22 Lions Publishing, 2020.

Table of Contents

Copyright Page 1

Book Reviews. 3

Introduction 5

Chapter 1: Why Do We Quit Dreaming? 7

Chapter 2: Why You Shouldn't Ask for Advice? 11

Chapter 3: Why is Jealousy a Powerful Mind Control Mechanism? 13

Chapter 4: Why Do People Give Up On Being Happy? 15

Chapter 5: Why Can't We Win This Psychosocial War? 17

Chapter 6: How to Overcome Our Paradigms? 21

Chapter 7: The Questioning of The Power Structure! 23

Chapter 8: The Returning of Christ and the Age of Aquarius. 25

Chapter 9: The Spiritual Implications in Our Perceptions of Reality. 29

Chapter 10: How Chaos Leads to Control? 31

Chapter 11: Why God is Everywhere and Has No Religion. 35

Chapter 12: Religious Hypocrisy is Everywhere! 39

Chapter 13: The Illuminati and The Mark of the Beast. 43

Chapter 14: The System of The New World Order. 47

Chapter 15: The Utopia of The New World Order. 49

Chapter 16: Hell on Earth. 53

Chapter 17: The Darkness of the Power Elite. 57

Chapter 18: How is the Mass Deception Kept Hidden? 61

Chapter 19: The History of the Big Illusion. 65

Chapter 20: The Portal to the Truth. 69

Chapter 21: The Truth Uniting All Faiths. 71

Chapter 22: How to Investigate the Truth? 73

Chapter 23: The Secret Within Humanity. 75

Chapter 24: The Importance of a Religious Education. 77

Chapter 25: Why Religion Always Degenerates. 81

Chapter 26: The Legacy of Jesus. 83

Chapter 27: The Greatest Secrets Never Told. 85

Chapter 28: Angels and Demons. 87

Copyright Page

Technocracy: The New World Order of the Illuminati and The Battle Between Good and Evil

By Dan Desmarques

Copyright © Dan Desmarques, 2012 (1st Ed.) All Rights Reserved.

Copyright © Dan Desmarques, 2014 (2nd Ed.) All Rights Reserved.

Copyright © Dan Desmarques, 2014 (3rd Ed.) All Rights Reserved.

Copyright © Dan Desmarques, 2015 (4th Ed.) All Rights Reserved.

Copyright © Dan Desmarques, 2020 (5th Ed.) All Rights Reserved.

Book Reviews.

These are some of the hundreds of positive reviews that the original version of this book has received since it was published:

"This book stretched my thinking and awareness, far more than I would expect." —Marlowe Aster, PhD

"This guy's books are very documentary film worthy" —Jake Coulter

"If you are not afraid, read it! Profound in its simplicity. Unique and truthful with no reservations" —Russ Watkins

"The most true book I have ever read" —Ashley Smith

"Easy to understand and loaded with interesting information that is easy to assimilate." —Michael Kempf

"I like the author's explanation of what the illuminati is, not the nonsense we read about devil worshippers. Definitely a good read." —Kwena Sibande

"Best thing I bought. It opened my eyes about many things, especially about my life and how wrongly I was living. I truly loved it. I am recommending it to everyone. God bless the author!" —Tomas Mik

"Inspiring and eye-opening to say the very least! Great read!" —Emily Triplett

"Very insightful! Thank you for sharing this with humanity!" —Derek Carlson

"Very knowledgeable and contains truthful information." —Tanya Kennedy

Introduction.

Did you know that you were programmed to be who you are at this moment, with all of your predicted successes and failures?

"Civilizations have been born and completed and then forgotten again and again. There is nothing new under the sun. What is has been. All that we learn and discover has existed before" (Colonel James Churchward, Freemason). However, "each generation imagines itself to be more intelligent than the one that went before it, and wiser than the one that comes after it" (George Orwell, Freemason).

This said, it is possible that you have been able to, somehow, challenge the orthodoxy of the system in which you were raised, by achieving results that weren't expected in your lifetime, while complying to many others that you weren't in favor of, and yet you surely didn't transform anything enough, or you would lose friends, relatives, jobs and even the opportunity of a love life.

"Anyone who challenges the prevailing orthodoxy finds himself silenced with surprising effectiveness. A genuinely unfashionable opinion is almost never given a fair hearing" (George Orwell, Freemason).

In this book, you will learn why the structure of mass thinking keeps you imprisoned to a reality that is far from your ideal potential. This book has been an Amazon Best Seller for more than eight years in a row, although previously published under other titles.

There have been many attempts at removing the original version of this book from the market, but if you are reading these words, the opportunity to obtain this extremely valuable information is still and surely within your reach.

Chapter 1: Why Do We Quit Dreaming?

Do you remember quitting your dreams? It was supposed to happen.

Any advice received from people around you, especially those who love you the most, were fabricated to make you follow the same mind programming in which you and them are included, and so that nobody gets out of it.

Hollywood and the music industry certainly play an important role here, by promoting artists, art and movies, that push forward messages reinforcing the idealization and worshipping of values which eventually become the belief-system of the masses.

Mankind is within a permanent psychological and spiritual warfare, in which the institutions that should be working for our well-being, are actually working towards the manipulation of our thoughts and decisions, in order to make us predictable and useful to the elites but stupid for ourselves at the same time. Smart enough to obey but too stupid to disobey effectively.

This couldn't be more obvious than what we see with modern psychology and psychiatry, which are almost entirely based on mind control and the destruction of the identity of the individual as an independent thinking organism.

The word "psy" means soul, or reason to breathe, and yet, the sciences including these three letters in their name, not only oppose the idea of soul, but do their best to destroy any soulful life purpose.

The collective always assumes the priority in any study, even when this collective is being deceived. And how can the collective deceive the individual? Through communication.

"If thought corrupts language, language can also corrupt thought" (George Orwell, Freemason), and that's how the sentences heard since we were born — from parents, teachers, neighbors and friends — as well as the ideas strongly imposed by the media, conditioned the way we think as individuals.

This programming is so strong and deep that ends up interfering with our own emotions and affecting our personality.

The soul then becomes suppressed by its own egotistical needs and desires, due to fear of scarcity and a competitive, although previously conditioned, thought pattern.

When people claim not to know what their life purpose is, despite reading many books about it, they're neglecting the need for compassion and love as a prerequisite to find such life purpose. And this compassion and love that I am talking about, starts with the self.

You can only break free from the emotional traps mentioned when you are courageous enough to confront them. But how useful it is when you read books or listen to speakers that are conditioned by the same paradigm?

"If the blind lead the blind, both fall into the same pit" (The Bible, Matthew 15:14).

A truly free thought pattern cannot fear itself. For to love freedom is to love oneself and his life, and "there is no fear in love, as fear has to do with punishment" (The Bible, John 4:18).

An artist is useful when his art elevates others;

A business person enriches by being useful to many;

A worker is needed when enriching someone;

A spiritual activity is effective when needed;

A religion is pertinent when effective.

All of human activities must be interrelated by means bridging effectiveness, need, enrichment, usefulness and progress. Or, as Hermes Trismegistus said, they must be "above, as they show themselves below".

This is why art is the best judge of the level of the masses in their path to enlightenment. For its inner value won't be perceived by those who labor with their body and in hunger unless they are conscious enough to see it as a means their personal elevation. Music, statues, and any other form of art that is widely accessible to the masses, must necessarily include codes, vibrations and concepts that inspire, propel one to dream and reinforce the witness of the art-form on the idea that he or she is capable of anything that he or she might see and want.

Art then has to be perverted and corrupted too for that to never occur. For when a mason can become a spiritual leader by choice, he cannot be controlled by any other means except the word of God.

The suffering of many occurs when this cycle has been broken by corrupt ideals and values, which redirect the soul downwards. That is the moment when their life purpose has been lost. For this life purpose is always related to a collective.

When one does not see his life purpose as related to the collective, he or she will not ever find it either.

Chapter 2: Why You Shouldn't Ask for Advice?

The worse advice ever that anyone can give to others, consists in telling them to ask a close relative or friend for opinions on a business idea, career or love partner.

The idea of scarcity made people extremely jealous of each other. Women in particular. Because scarcity boosts the economy. It creates in people the need to purchase in abundance and worship those who have money as a way to make them focus on productivity more than their own emotions.

This tactic works, as it made most people assume that the value of an individual is measured by how much he possesses or the value of his possessions.

We can't blame them for it, however, as they were never given any other form of social worth measurement.

Those are the values that the system promotes to sustain itself and grow. People need to believe in such things for the system in which they live to survive and the elites at the top to prosper.

Few realize, however, that this jealousy doesn't change when inside the family or among best friends. And I could go deeper and discuss egotistical needs and mainstream psychology, but I don't even have to. Because, generally speaking, people will never tell you anything that makes you end up better than them.

It is like when you want to start a business or change country. Everyone warns you about the dangers and the challenges, and the impossibilities, because, if you succeed, they will feel horrible with themselves, and the fact that they may have neglected the same opportunities in the past.

Their mind has been programmed to oppose any sense of inferiority and compete within their environment. That is why you should never ask anyone else what they think of your decisions.

I've actually lost many friends recently like that. They would tell me to dump my girlfriend. And the women were even far more aggressive than the men.

They also tried to convince me to exchange my former partners for one their own friends instead. And would get angry whenever I refused, and insult me in return.

That is when I realized how aggressive women can be in destroying the relationships of their own friends. For even if one of my relationships wasn't going well, they had no right to tell me to end it or to cheat. But they did, and very aggressively.

Can you guess what happened in this particular case? That girlfriend fell for the same trap and did what her own friends said — which was the same I heard, and cheated. And so, I had to end it. In the end, I was forced to end it anyway.

I don't regret anything because I had to keep myself faithful to my own values, but that cost me a relationship and many friendships.

Now, why were her friends so full of hate and jealousy? Because if that girl remained with me, she wouldn't need to work anymore and could simply enjoy life by traveling the world. That was too unbearable to hear for those who are stuck to jobs they hate and may remain so until they die.

This competitive attitude becomes even more ridiculous when people fear asking for help to those who have accomplished what they want, as when someone tells me, 'I can't ask you how to write a book because you are a writer, and therefore, you are my competitor'.

I have published close to four hundred books. How exactly is this person planning to compete against that if she can't even finish one?

I would have to be very greedy to refuse passing such advice and she would have to assume my greediness to receive none. But that's exactly what happens when people live within a competitive mindset. They fight against each other and achieve very little on their own.

That is exactly the state of mind that the elites want for the masses, as it makes it easier to keep them under control. For "men are not prisoners of fate, but only prisoners of their own minds" (Franklin D. Roosevelt, Freemason).

Chapter 3: Why is Jealousy a Powerful Mind Control Mechanism?

Jealousy is obvious but you do need experience to see it.

People are often blinded by their fears. And jealousy is a form of fear that preys on the fear of others. Fear needs companionship. If are afraid of nothing, others will fear your lack of fear.

Just imagine the following situation: A woman meets a man she really likes. He is everything she ever dreamed. And so, she will naturally start to glow of happiness.

This happiness will be hard to hide. And will have effects on her social surroundings. Her friends will start searching for flaws, where they can push for the destruction of that happiness. Except that, rather than a fight, this will seem like a friendly conversation. They may ask, "what type of car does he drive?" or "Why doesn't he have a car?"

Now, why would they ask such questions? Because if the woman found a man that is traveling the whole world, he obviously won't have a car, because he doesn't need one. And as if the fact that he is wealthy enough to go where he wants on the entire planet wasn't obvious enough, and the car is the true measurement of his possessions.

Misery always need companionship too. Therefore it is easy to project these feelings on others to keep them under our radar.

This is how women's best friends destroy their life and keep them miserable.

It's always easy to find companions to get drunk and forget misery but you will rarely find companionship in your road to success.

People also don't like change, and when you change, you will change them by default. Therefore, they don't want your changes to be superior to their previous perceptions, otherwise their self-perception in relation to the perceptions they made of you, will change as well.

Whenever you change too much and too fast, you always risk losing most of your friendships and even marriage.

As a matter of fact, most divorces are initiated because one of the partners felt somehow depreciated and devalued in the relationship.

Why is then that people tend to repeat their experiences? Because the image of themselves did not change after they change partner.

Chapter 4: Why Do People Give Up On Being Happy?

Why would a woman, for example, give up on a man that makes her extremely happy?

If she spends most of her time complaining to her friends about an ex-husband or other men she slept with, then that is what their friends basically become: companions of misery.

What will happen if she then tells them that she met a man that makes her extremely happy and is completely different from all others she met before? They will convince her to leave him.

We can say that love blinds everyone, even the most wise, reason why we need friends to keep us aware of the dangers. But how useful is that motto, when we can't see if our friends are truly helping us or keeping us miserable?

In other words, if you need your friends to help you make decisions, you are not mature enough to know what love truly is. Because they can only convince you to abandon a good decision when you are not mature enough to know that you must keep it and persist with it.

Now, the question is, how can people convince somebody to abandon a partner that makes them happy and fulfills their requirements and needs?

That is actually very easy. Just consider the things you are afraid. Is it being cheated? Being abandoned? Being controlled? Being manipulated? Being lied to? Because, first, your friends find your fears and then use them against you.

There is another technique to accomplish the same result. And it's the opposite. It is the idea that you can find better.

How many times you heard this one: "I know a guy that is much richer, more handsome, and more successful, than the one you met"? Or, for example, "thousands of guys want you, and you're struggling with that one. Why? You are just wasting your time".

In business, that's called overpricing or overvaluing a product, depending on the situation of the market and what we wish to accomplish. But, the truth is, many people have this issue, and women in particular. They easily overvalue themselves because they have many guys texting them messages and pressing 'like' on half naked photos.

Then, they wonder why they keep sleeping with the cat every night.

A woman who is beautiful but emotional abusive, for example, keeps nobody. But what will her friends say? "You are so hot, you can get any guy you want."

Yes, get, not keep.

The same applies to a career or a business. Working hard and many hours is not the same as improving and going somewhere.

Most people are merely going in circles and exhausting themselves to death. But they love to use the words: "I'm busy!"

Chapter 5: Why Can't We Win This Psychosocial War?

It is extremely difficult to win in this psychosocial war that has been imposed on us. Knowledge, life experience and potential or competence won't change our outcome, unless we are strong enough to accomplish our results despite the necessary solitude and the amount of betrayals we may have to experience.

What was once a condition of leadership is now becoming the mainstream to anyone who wishes to be successful in life. Because, the more the majority struggles to blend with the majority and be like the majority, the more being different becomes the ultimate challenge.

Most people assume that because I am more knowledgeable, I should also be more accomplished in my social dynamics, but I will explain to you why it isn't so with an example that happened to me.

I met a Ukrainian girl in Poland and she was beautiful. I really liked her, although she seemed to like me a lot more. She said I was everything she was looking for and thought would never find. She also said I was more mature and wise than any other man she met before. But guess what her friends used to destroy her newest relationship? Exactly that! They told her the following: "If he is very smart, he is probably manipulating you."

How do I know? Because, suddenly, the fact that I was smart became a big problem for her. She would constantly ask me, in the form of an assumption: "I hope you are not manipulating me just because you know more than me. Are you?"

What could I say that would remove the poison from inside of her? Virtually nothing.

Her friends kept poisoning her until she decided to end everything. And people do follow the advice that has a stronger emotional component.

We are fundamentally emotional beings, but emotions without proper reasoning do make us stupid. And to choose friendships over love is always stupid, especially when this love leads us to our goals — a family, a trustworthy partner and dream lifestyle.

It's not possible to win this war when it has been promoted from birth.

You have to literally work your way out of it, by getting informed and confronting yourself with the facts. And maybe even changing your priorities in life and the way you look at yourself.

Every time you ask others for advice, it is as if you were walking backwards in life.

I can tell the difference between an independent idea and a parasitic idea, but most people can't. They allow themselves to be sucked in into the storms of misunderstanding, fear and jealousy.

I'm not saying, however, that people don't have their own fears too. If a person tells you that she doesn't trust someone who wears glasses, was born in a certain country, or has a certain job, that is something they have to live with, and is not related to you.

Whenever a woman tells me that my career was a wrong choice, I can only laugh at her, and for three reasons:

1. She doesn't have any idea of how much money I make, which makes her arguments useless;

2. She is positioning her self-worth above mine, which means she will never get my respect because she will never respect me either;

3. She has no right to tell others what is right or wrong, and will most likely live a miserable life, for the simple fact that you can't always have what you want, and failure is a precondition to success. You can only not fail by doing nothing.

Even though these situations are becoming increasingly common, we can't really apologize or feel guilty for rejecting such people.

At very least, we must acknowledge the fact that the value of a human life has been decreasing and rapidly. The imbecility of many is making their own death a very small price — a small loss for humanity.

An holocaust today doesn't have the same implications that it would have decades ago.

When people analyze reality as if others were just objects, they objectivity themselves, and by default, they make themselves transitory, replaceable and, at one point in time, useless as well.

Personally, I don't understand why so many people, who barely read anything in their entire life, don't learn from anyone, don't spend any time debating different ideas, want to call themselves open-minded, just because it sounds good to say it.

If a person doesn't know much, calling herself open-minded is irrelevant.

When a billionaire gives one percent of his wealth to charity, this person is giving quite a lot of money. When the common person gives one percent, he isn't giving much, and won't make any difference.

The same with being open-minded. An idiot who is open-minded is still an idiot you can't learn from or talk with without facing tremendous challenges whenever opinions diverge.

An open mind with nothing inside is as good as a close mind.

Chapter 6: How to Overcome Our Paradigms?

One of the purposes of this book is to show you a path beyond the paradigm that conditions us from birth. Because only then we can begin deprograming ourselves.

Once the deprograming happens, the true soul of the individual is revealed. And upon the imminence of such awareness, it is possible to develop a higher understanding in regards to the universal truth, and change life as much as we want it to be changed.

The direct connection with the divine, seen by many secret societies as a true state of enlightenment, permits one to stretch his thinking capacity and become more profound in observing reality. When this occurs, we experience the uncovering of many truths, as if a veil had fallen before our eyes.

We are now living in the Age of Aquarius, and "as Aquarius is an airy, scientific and intellectual sign, the New Faith for this age must be rooted in reason" (Max Heindel, Rosicrucian Fellowship). This is why the prophecy of anyone who once described the Era of Aquarius, is rooted in the alchemical transformation of consciousness and the revolution of thought in the direction of a whole new world.

Based on such writings, and taking into consideration the amount of information presented here, and the level of simplification applied, this is surely one of the most empowering, complete and uplifting books you will ever read in your entire life about gaining wealth, power and health, using the law of attraction and the power of thought when combined with the right values.

Nonetheless, this book doesn't intend to explore or make use of the knowledge of secret societies in a way that can make it be misinterpreted, but neither exalts them with a dogmatic approach.

It must be known that, although many of the most influential and powerful people in history, and in the fields of art, music, politics and religion, were linked to secret societies, and ended up promoting, as well as indirectly allowing, the formation of what today is known as the Power Elite, there isn't necessarily a direct link between both outcomes. This, as much as in the valley of the blind the one-eyed man is king.

In other words, those to whom we now call the Power Elite, the Illuminati, the Watchers, the 1%, aren't as enlightened as you would feel if holding a torch in the middle of a dark and wild forest.

Although it may be true that the knowledge that these individuals possess is directly linked to the power, wealth, creativity and the influence that they have accumulated, it is also directly correlated with the enormous level of ignorance that the rest of the world has become accustomed to experience as a routine and to call normal.

This said, they are as evil as the teeth of a hungry crocodile inside a river with swimmers. Which is the same as to say that they have acquired as much power as we allowed them to have, without evaluating their character or even caring about the outcome.

The natural preponderance of the human race to desire power over others and to admire such power, is what leads us to a social structure that favors some over others.

The division of the world in a pyramidal structure of power isn't an artificial construct as much as it is a natural correspondence to a tendency on the human race to worship and follow.

The same occurs in the relation between those who desire power over others and the ones who neglect knowing and interfering in the life of the ones who exercise such power. Or the fact that, those at the top, can always and easily manipulate the masses who obsess over exterior representations of value rather than internal ones.

If arrogance becomes more important than humility and kindness, and perceived power becomes more important than inherent intellectual power, then a fool can easily rule over many fools.

Chapter 7: The Questioning of The Power Structure!

Our fellow man has learned to hate his brothers and sisters, worship authority, reject knowledge and wisdom, and embrace animalistic predispositions, such as anger, violence, competition, laziness, lust and hate. And, in this sense, we can say that humanity has done its best in empowering humans with the truth that they reject.

Could the ones who praise themselves of a higher moral, due to the religion they follow, be any different?

No, and for these exact same reasons. Whenever you consider yourself morally superior and entitled to more than others, you are, by default, justifying the type of system that surrounds you, even if you believe to oppose it.

Either through authoritarian or revolutionary actions, nearly nothing was truly obtained for the future of the human race, except for a potential for freedom that this same race neglects, misuses and rejects. And there is nothing we can do against human stupidity, which is as dangerous as the power that it has permitted for some men in the world to rise above others.

It must be remembered that Mao, Stalin and Hitler did not force themselves to power. They convinced the masses to give them such power, by offering solutions that these masses desperately needed, even if to solve problems they themselves created.

It is here that books like this one assume a major importance, not in presenting something that the Power Elite already knows, but in allowing those who aren't part of it, to have a better and more profound insight and understanding of the universal truths.

This, so that they too may be able to see the world as it is, behind the curtains of neurotic beliefs of the lost and that were purposely created to further enrich and empower the social structure that we already have.

Most of our beliefs of today are nothing more that a certification of status. The two concepts are correlated. As soon as your status or beliefs change, you will necessarily change too within the world you know.

That is why, either a perception of higher status of beliefs, are crucial if you wish to change your fate.

You can focus on one or the other but you can't neglect either in this process.

Chapter 8: The Returning of Christ and the Age of Aquarius.

There is this delusional idea that Christians will save the world, when this is very unlikely to happen.

The vast majority of the Christians I have met during my lifetime, and from different religions, are actually happy and eager for the world to end, as they believe that, in the last days, Christ returns to Earth to save them.

This is a very selfish viewpoint on the outcome of things but extremely common as well.

Life is so unbearable and difficult, that most, in reality, wish these things to happen.

In a strange way, they end up promoting these things too, through apathetic behavior and a pro-apocalypse attitude.

In other words, they oppose the coming of Christ in their heart, by being resentful and egotistical in regards to the situation of the world. And because of that, they develop an aggressive attitude towards those who question their dogmas too much, which is also, in itself, and anti-christian behavior.

In psychology, this is called a self-fulfilling prophecy: When we oppose something and then become what we oppose by reflecting what we wish to reject.

What I am trying to say here, is that the coming of Christ is a metaphor for the christ-like compassion that we need in order to transition to a higher spiritual realm.

In truth, the Era of Aquarius represents an awakening, in which we start to question our values and embrace the need for more love and compassion for each other and life in general.

Whenever we secretly and willingly hope for an apocalypse to occur, just because we consider ourselves above the consequences, we are, by focusing more on the possibility than the solutions, becoming as the ones we oppose. And that is the greatest spiritual secret that the Age of Aquarius reveals.

Furthermore, as we approach this Age, we should be noticing a faster correlation between cause and effect, actions and karmic consequences, as well as a greater perception of how we project our own nature unto others.

Yes, I am referring here to the end of duality as we knew it for many thousands of years.

As we move onwards to that stage, we will see that the difficulty in solving complex problems is more related to the limitations of the human mind and not so much a problem in itself.

Mankind developed by possessing a dual perception of reality, which was strengthened and used against itself, through the indoctrination of the educational system: right and wrong; true and false; correct and incorrect. Now, we need to overcome it.

Most people are unable to perceive solutions to problems through a complexity of measures and angles. But this situation created a huge gap between what the mind perceives and what the spirit feels. Because the human mind has been trapped even though the state of the spirit was always evolving.

In secret societies, this is called a crystallization, and often warns of an upcoming catastrophe that ends the spiritual and mental stagnation.

The symptoms of this stagnation are, however, already present. People started suffering more from anxiety, fear, depression and uncontrollable anger. And the psychiatric interference to suppress even more these states of unrest, are part of another mechanic of the system in an attempt to control itself.

Such differentiation between spirit and beliefs, however, can't last for too long. It comes a point in which the system in itself collapses, and rapidly. Because it wasn't able to adjust to the transitions that the energy field required.

This collapse, naturally, occurs first within the human mind, reason why it seems that as we approach the Age of Aquarius, people seem to start acting more irrational, confused and impulsively. Yes, people are more insane and narcissistic today, because they are also divided between opposing realities. They are lost. Their identity has been hijacked.

The need for an identity in the dark always causes a tremendous anxiety. And when people are anxious, but unaware of the way out, they will do anything to calm such emotion. Even if what they do makes no sense, such as blaming the wrong people and attacking themselves.

This situation was perfectly visible during the COVID-19 outbreak in which the majority was fighting over toilet paper and insulting the scientists who tried to explain the problem from a different angle than their politicians wished to follow, which was a global lockdown of the population.

Somehow, being in house arrest, made much more sense to the population. And they even tried to control those who attempted to refuse such rules.

The COVID-19 pandemic proved, above anything, that mass stupidity always rules over intellect.

Chapter 9: The Spiritual Implications in Our Perceptions of Reality.

When someone explains to us a complexity of approaches, such as when referring to the immune system, for example, we become confused. We want direct answers. And they do not exist, because the world does not function like that.

The need for a direct answer is always a need to satisfy an innate state of imbecility — a linear approach on reality.

That linear approach to the truth is also reflection of an egotistical and limiting view on reality, albeit related to what we were indoctrinated to assume.

Intelligence is then, the ability to move from a certain level of complexity to a higher one. It is the movement from one approach to many, from the physical to the abstract, from the simple to the complex, from the need to control one aspect of reality to the embracing of chaos.

The economic system requires this same type of approach.

We can't always use the same vocabulary when moving from one field to another. And for this reason, we can't expect an expert in one field to give us answers related to another. This type of approach necessarily requires a synergy of intellects. And, because the educational system taught the majority to compete rather than cooperate, most people are unaware of this simple fact.

They can navigate through their own field of knowledge but struggle when transferring their thinking process to another, for lack of vocabulary and a lack of perception of reality from that different viewpoint.

This type of organization made sure that nobody is able to easily accumulate the totality of the data needed to be able to give a more detailed approach to a certain field, either it is economical, political or medical.

This does apply to spirituality as well. Very few people can merge a vast diversity of religious approaches.

Whenever you try to explain to them how to do it, they will ridicule such attempt and call it cherry picking. Because their brain is simply not capable of understanding your explanation. They are too far from that possibility.

Now, you place these same individuals before a reality they can't comprehend and they panic. This applies to a new pandemic, proof of alien life, or even me as an individual.

I am capable of so many different things, that most people simply refuse to believe that I am real. They refuse to believe that I possess so much knowledge, they refuse to believe that I have written so many books, they refuse to, fundamentally, accept that I am part of their reality.

The more I try to explain myself, and the more honest I am in my explanations, the more insults I get. Because that's how people protect themselves from truths they can't assimilate.

Assimilating such truths by force would collapse the entirety of their belief-system, which is based on lies.

If you transfer this situation to a type of pandemic that nobody has ever encountered before, it leads to mass fear and hysteria. After all, doctors don't know what to do in order to save their patients, politicians don't know what to do to maintain the economy going, and people don't know what to do to survive.

It is the perfect chaos that allows controlling the masses. And this is why whatsoever was ordered during the COVID-19 epidemic, was promptly obeyed by nearly eight billion humans.

It is interesting to see how you can control so many people through ignorance and fear.

In situations of mass panic and confusion, chaos thrives, but from this chaos a new order also appears, often brought forward by new leaders that seem to be more insightful than the masses. And who could lead the masses out of chaos better than the ones who promoted it?

Chapter 10: How Chaos Leads to Control?

For the common mortal to analyze reality at the level of an elite member of society — the so called illuminati — this person would have to possess the same amount of information, which is not possible when all the channels are filtering it, hiding it and blocking it, and even shaming the ones who try to study it.

Social media now insists on labeling anything related to inconvenient truths, or simply truths outside of what is mainstream and officially accepted, as "false news" or "conspiracy theories", when all you need is a deeper investigation to see how they distort many truths to place them under the categories of false or lie.

Very few people dare to even do such analysis. The majority is too afraid of ridicule and don't consider themselves able enough to analyze such a level of contradictions.

In many cases, they don't even possess enough time, self-respect or empathy for others, to care. And this is precisely why it is so easy to disperse mass opinion, create conflicts inside society, and then redirect the masses as if they were nothing more than sheep.

Most people will never consider an hypothesis that wasn't accepted by the source which they consider to be an authority on their reasoning. They don't really trust their own intelligence enough to question such authority, because they were never thought on how to think independently.

One of the most common mistakes that I see people doing in relation to this topic is to assume that everyone has an opinion and all opinions are important. This attitude creates a separation between the dumb idiots and the ones who come from an authoritarian position, as if having an opinion was the same as developing a conclusion based on facts. And this, while neglecting any reasoning.

Most people have no clue, whatsoever, about how to differentiate an opinion from a properly organized and facts-based argument. But even more serious than this, is that they have no clue about the difference between a biased research (i.e., when a research is manipulated to prove an hypothesis) and a non-biased research (such as when a research is hidden from the public because it contradicts an agenda).

The socialist approach to reality with a communist taste to it is far from corresponding to a pattern of analysis that could allow reaching for the truth. Because, whenever everything can be relativized, anything can be easily invalidated as well.

There is no such thing as an opinion, ego or assumptions, when we are referring to the one truth. For it is always correct and due to these very same reasons exposed here.

Those who overlook the deeper meaning of the words emerging from the ones who have been immersed in its realm, will also lose the opportunity to heal themselves. Because such words contain emotions arranged as codes to bridge the soul towards a unity, commonly known as God, and in doing so, raise consciousness to higher levels.

As a collective, we can indeed elevate ourselves, if we practice the art of thinking and reasoning according to a compassionate and effective purpose.

You can actually break the phrases of the most high in parts, to see pyramids, alchemical equations and pentagrams within their structures. For all follow the same lineage of those who have come before them and as them did the same.

We are all students of the same spiritual school, one that remains invisible to those who are not allowed to enter, an eternal school without a name or a location, unlocked through the heart and welcomed through the pineal gland.

This greatest secret, however, is not in the process but rather the circumstances dictated from above and which the masses typically wish to avoid. Such circumstances, albeit outside conscious control, crucify the enlightened to a lifetime of scorn, hatred and resentment, in which personal will is exchanged for the salvation of the many.

This metaphor has been taken to extremes by Christian scholars but is still present through many famous figures, including the most recent in human history; and is not determined by religious beliefs, origins or cultures.

Everyone who has embraced the same school, experienced the same circumstances and has went through the same process, experiences detachment and discrimination.

The ultimate purpose, if aligned with Divine will, is to create a better understanding of the meaning of synergy, commonly know as love, while fulfilling a spiritual purpose aligned with faith.

Very little, if anything, can be done amidst a world of mass ignorance, without a tremendous faith. But faith without the right knowledge is self-deceptive foolishness.

The vast majority of the religious congregations of the world are nothing more than communities of fools, because they don't practice the art of thinking in alignment with the truth. They can be easily corrupted, even when possessing the right books, and indeed, they've all been corrupted.

Chapter 11: Why God is Everywhere and Has No Religion.

The one and true God has no religion. He is everywhere, because His truth is dispersed and arranged according to the capacity of the faith seekers.

This is well explained in "The Gospel of the Twelve", when Tomas asks to Jesus:

— "What is the truth, if the same things present themselves differently to different individuals, and even to the same minds at different times?"

Jesus answers him the following:

— "The truth is revealed according to your ability to understand it and assimilate it.

The one truth is revealed in many perspectives, and while some see only one, others can only see another; and some people see more than others, as they are allowed to see, according to their moral conduct.

The truth is then to each individual as the separate understanding perceives it at that time until a higher truth is manifested to that person; and to souls who are in a position to receive higher light, more light is given to them. But if you wish to make others see the truth only as you see it, and beyond that no other, then you have no love, and without love, faith is dead. For love is the fulfillment of the law, and the law is above all human error."

This was how Jesus explained that, while those who consider themselves morally superior and the atheists hide from their own fears, allowing their faith or beliefs to be shaken, compromised and ridiculed, or stopped, if necessary, through different means of censorship, either online or offline, those who understand God from this multifaceted viewpoint, see in any relationship developed a path of light. And that is why they can meditate anywhere and at any moment, and feel this deep connection.

Those who are too attached to their own beliefs, religious books and dogmas, may never understand this message of Christ. And that is also why they can be easily deceived or changed through fear, and manipulated through their own understanding of the truth.

I must also add that fear is a precursor to evil. When you allow fear to consume your heart, you allow the real temple of God to be contaminated by darkness and egotism.

The light won't enter and self-destruction will follow. Reason why the one who wishes to vanquish darkness in times of major deceit has to necessarily act as a warrior, a knight at the service of a superior force.

Being a Knight Templar, according to this principle, is then not a condition attributed to you by history or cults, but rather one you own by yourself, through ethical value. Because the Temple has always been within you and the spiritual war has always been imposed upon you too. It chooses no gender or location. It is forced on all and every single person.

Due to this fact, which many exorcists have struggled to comprehend for thousands of years, when you enter a door to a physical temple, you are actually entering the door to your own spiritual temple. Only then you understand what is to pray in the privacy of your mind while ignoring symbols and expectations.

Very few people can see this door, and worship God beyond symbols and temples. And I find it interesting, when friends say to me: "You have the right qualities to be a muslim; You should read the Quran and consider joining this religion";

Or when they say: "You speak like a true buddhist, you should come to our meetings whenever you have the chance";

Or, "you fit perfectly well in what the bible describes that a good christian should be and do, and I really hope you become one of us";

Or, "you already know too much to be a freemason, but you should certainly join our group to meet more people like you";

Or, "you know so much about Rosicrucianism and the Pythagorean Brotherhood, that you must have been a Knight Templar in a previous life";

Or, "you match exactly what our founder said about a real spiritual being, and you would be happy to work in Scientology with us".

Some readers even told me: "I started reading your books because I found true Satanism in your words, and I'm a devoted Satanist for many years".

Again and again, people insist on viewing reality from their own perspective, not knowing that I am seeing it from all these angles and far more.

There is only one truth. All paths lead to it.

It is like playing music live. You don't really think about the music as much as you think of the experience being offered. Some like the music and others don't. Some may think the music is aggressive, and others energetic. Some feel joy and others may feel anger. But, ultimately, you want to elevate people to a higher ground, where they see and feel differently, and that state must be better than the previous where they found themselves before.

The label attributed to it or even the title of the book that can cause it doesn't truly matter here. It matters only that they are evolving upwards and towards a higher consciousness, where they then understand the importance of compassion, kindness, wisdom and truth.

Chapter 12: Religious Hypocrisy is Everywhere!

Just as our perspectives of the one truth, so our world is also more complex than it seems.

The religious groups that actually intervene the most against the governments end up in the shadows. Most people have never heard of such groups.

In some cases, the groups have such a bad reputation, that it becomes hard to believe they may have a positive intervention in the fate of mankind.

Scientology, for example, through Narconon, provides an excellent aid to those who suffer from drug addiction, and with far more positive results than any other institution. And, through the Citizens Commission on Human Rights, they have helped many parents get their children back, after the psychiatric industry took them away to enforce psychiatric drugs.

Nevertheless, they are one of the most ridiculed and discriminated religions. Although I can't say for no reason.

I have reported several Scientologists to their leaders for breaking their own ethical codes and literally insulting me with lies, and those reports never got even an investigation.

Many Scientologists actually violently attack and persecute anyone who questions their authority and morals. Even though many of them have none. By violating their own ethical codes, they end up justifying being labeled as a dangerous and crazy cult.

They do have ethical codes and encyclopedias filled with them. They simply ignore all of that because they consider themselves to be too superior to common humans to be judged, even when the facts are overwhelming with proves of slander and criminal activities, as was the case of a Scientologist I encountered in Lithuania — the leader of Scientology in that country.

You look at their books about what a criminal is — and which according to them is an antisocial personality, or an SP (Suppressive Person) — and then you compare their behaviors, and interestingly find most of them to fit perfectly well into those descriptions.

You then wonder, how is it possible that they slander themselves when projecting fault on others?

I sent a report about this Jurgita of Lithuania to the Headquarters in Denmark, and merely got three promises of investigations that never truly occurred. They also never corrected me because I was right on every single point I accused her of and had many proves as well. But, you see, when there is too much money to be made, religion goes down the toilet and everything is valid.

Success then becomes a measurement of how much money is made rather than how many people were insulted with lies, and how much bullshit was told that even violates Scientology itself. Somehow, the Scientologists of today think they have the right to literally violate everything the founder created, just because they entered his domain.

They are also more concerned about how to make people pay more for common sense, than actually providing anything useful to anyone who is not enslaved by their organization. And then wonder how is it possible that I know a lot much more than their higher ranks.

Somehow, all religious groups consider themselves superior to the rest, even though they never investigated enough to make a proper judgement, and neither do they possess the capacity or interest to do such analysis.

It must also be said that, the Christians of today, have nearly nothing to do with the Christians who followed Christ. They are more concerned with dying than getting information or passing on information.

This is the real problem with modern christianity. It has turned into a religion of a mass but delusional sheep-like mentality.

Besides these facts, there is also too much misinformation to confuse people. Mainly promoted by journalists who do not understand anything about the subject of world control and desperately want to appear as experts in the field, to save their own careers and gain popularity with shortcuts and shocking news.

The truth is that terms like "conspiracy theory" and "illuminati", or even the blaming of Freemasons and other specific religious groups or cults, is an old tactic, developed by the communists and then used by the CIA to confuse people and prevent them from accessing the facts.

I seriously doubt that anyone would waste any time on Scientology if this organization was not so involved in fighting the Pharmaceutical Corporations, and in specific, the Psychiatric Industry and their abuses of the human rights.

I say this because you have far more lunatic organizations that everyone ignores, such as the Raelians, who rent entire hotel buildings for their "love parties" (also known as orgies).

Mankind is, to a great extent, hypocrite. And religions don't escape this domain of hypocrisy, no matter how pure and moral they want to appear to others.

The fact that many priests accused of pedophilia are able to continue with their life in secrecy and never face jail, shows us the state of the world we live in, for people can close their eyes to keep their own ceremonies going.

The Catholic church is just as hypocritical as its followers who don't put any pressure for the crimes committed to be punished.

Quite often, the masses only persecute a group when they want to fulfill their own agenda.

The use of Jews as scapegoats was exactly the same technique, applied to advance the agenda of the second world war.

In reality, many religions have disappeared like that. Just as in the past, with other wars the same has happened.

Chapter 13: The Illuminati and The Mark of the Beast.

The level of complexity in the world is so high, that most people want to simplify, especially the journalists who investigate these topics. And that's how they end up getting confused and confusing others in the process.

I say this to help you understand reality from a spiritual point of view. Because the Elite at the top is fundamentally composed by atheists, bureaucrats and technocrats, but more importantly, hypocrites of the highest order.

If you can see lack of morals in the lowest religious orders — offered to the masses — don't expect a special type of sophistication at the top — for the lunatics and psychopaths who rule the world — or as Dr. Syed Mujahid Kamran brilliantly put it: Satanic Psychopathic Brotherhood.

The parties, with statues and symbols, where they dance naked around fireplaces and sing absurdities, usually with masks, as with the case of Bohemian Grove or the Rothschild's private events (accurately represented in the movie Eyes Wide Shut), are created more for entertainment purposes than anything else.

That's why such parties are always filled with prostitutes. And I'm not referring only to common prostitutes, but all the actresses and singers who fucked their way to the top, and then decided to take revenge once they hit the wall and became too old to be part of anything in their industry.

Due to the fact that most of these groups are composed by influential and wealthy families, they like to portray themselves as very smart and enlightened. It is indeed to feel special in a world of fools. But many of them almost always stole the technology and resources from others and then patented everything under their own name.

They are, in a certain way, a type of modern pirates. They did nothing special or that justifies being special.

In the Documentary, "The One Percent", this fact is well stated by the producer — Jamie Johnson, when he shows through different, but properly organized interviews, that the main difference between them and the rest of the North Americans, comes in the form of opportunities that their families took by force, luck of criminal activities in the past, and that allowed them to maintain a certain social status ever since.

It is precisely because the vast majority of these families are composed by atheists and technocrats, that they end up behaving like psychopaths at some point — without empathy, and with an enormous pleasure for the control and abuse of others.

This is why we can't expect the mark of the beast — which Microsoft already patented through the code WO2020060606 — to be the real problem. But rather what it implies.

When allied with ID2020, which Bill Gates founded with the intention of creating a digital identification system, and a company named RFID-WIOT-SEARCH, whose website Facebook systematically stops from being shared, as well the 5G technology, creates the perfect prison planet, filled with microchipped slaves.

This isn't the crazier part. Microsoft patent 666 is a system that allows converting biometric activity into cryptocurrency. In other words, once you have the implant under your skin, you can be monitored by 5G, and you will only be paid according to what you do.

If you are not paid, you will not eat, because the RFID technology will be in all products that you consume.

In other words, the mark of the beast is not necessarily a mark in itself, but everything that it will do to you, and which can be resumed in turning you into a digitally-controlled-zombie. A cyborg, to be more precise.

That is what a separation from God really means. Once humans merge with Artificial Intelligence and become as machines, humanity ends. God is disconnected from the collective.

This God is then replaced by an artificial process, under the surveillance of a central and using radio-frequency technology, in what could be named as artificial telepathy.

This technology has been around for many years. People just don't know it.

In resume, if you can control a computer through thoughts, anyone can do the inverse and direct your thoughts through a computer.

If it is possible to control a machine using your mind, how hard do you think it is for a human-operated-machine to control your mind using 5G radio-frequency? And how difficult do you think it would be, if you actually implanted a chip inside your body?

Chapter 14: The System of The New World Order.

There is an immense technology and knowledge in the fields of medicine and science, which the vast majority of the population is unaware. Because what the Elite did was to divide the world:

To the ignorant, they created one way (the officially approved version of science and medicine);

And to themselves, they created another way (conducted through private investments and research).

The Rockefeller Foundation, for example, which started from the oil money of John D. Rockefeller, used it to buy out part of the massive German pharmaceutical cartel, I.G. Farben.

This was the very same cartel that would later assist Hitler to implement his eugenics-based vision of a New World Order founded on racial supremacy, by manufacturing chemicals and poisons for war.

"With the control of drug manufacturing under his wings, Rockefeller then embarked on a decidedly wicked plan – wicked from the point of view of a free and healthy humanity, but brilliant from a business perspective.

Rockefeller saw that there were many types of doctors and healing modalities in existence at that time, from chiropractic to naturopathy to homeopathy to holistic medicine to herbal medicine and more. He wanted to eliminate the competitors of western medicine (the only modality which would propose drugs and radiation as treatment, thus enriching Rockefeller who owned the means to produce these treatments), so he hired a man called Abraham Flexner to submit a report to Congress in 1910.

This report "concluded" that there were too many doctors and medical schools in America, and that all the natural healing modalities which had existed for hundreds or thousands of years were unscientific quackery. It called for the standardization of medical education, whereby only the allopathic-based AMA be allowed to grant medical school licenses in the US.

Sadly, Congress acted upon the conclusions and made them law. Incredibly, allopathy became the standard mainstream modality, even though its three main methods of treatment in the 1800s had been blood-letting, surgery and the injection of toxic heavy metals like lead and mercury to supposedly displace disease.

It should be noted that hemp was also demonized and criminalized not long after this, not because there is anything dangerous about it, but because it was a huge threat (as both medicine and fuel) to the Rockefeller drug and oil industries, respectively" (Makia Freeman, In thefreedomarticles.com).

This is why the masses today do not understand anything about the immune system, radiation, telepathy, mental health, mind control, etc. Humanity has been hijacked by what is termed bio-piracy.

What the masses get is merely a pathetic and primitive view of these subjects. Even the Universities are far from being able to conduct proper research in the field of health.

Not long ago, a friend of mine, who was a doctor in China, had her Ph.D. research paper rejected, because it was focused on Holistic Medicine. She was told that insisting on the topic could lead her to lose her license to practice medicine.

Chapter 15: The Utopia of The New World Order.

The Elite call themselves "The Illuminati", only because the majority of the population is ignorant of the scientific advances that have existed for decades.

The microchip — that the Rockefeller family, Bill Gates and Microsoft want to implant on the masses —, for example, has been in existence for many decades. It was brought out publicly by Harry Sockman in 1948.

However, it was only in 1963 that new ideas related to scattering data and information were formulated and implemented.

In 1977, the first RFID transmitting license plate is created, and in 2015, it was estimated that the RFID market could be valued at $26 billion. Although, with 5G technology and Artificial Intelligence, the value for this market has now reached the trillions of dollars.

On the 20th of June 2016, Tom Wheeler, as FFC (Federal Communications Commission) Chairman, said publicly — on the Future of Wireless Communication — the following:

"Autonomous vehicles will be controlled in the cloud. Smart-city energy grids, transportation networks, and water systems will be controlled in the cloud. Immersive education and entertainment will come from the cloud. (...)

Today's technology – 4G – completed the digital migration, enabling higher speeds for sophisticated applications including video. Again, greater capability led to unanticipated innovation: without 4G, there could be no WAZE, or Uber, or Snapchat, or Instagram.

Now, I've listed some examples of what 5G makes possible, but if anyone tells you they know the details of what 5G will deliver, walk the other way.

Yes, 5G will connect the Internet of Everything. If something can be connected, it will be connected in a 5G world. But with predictions of hundreds of billions of microchip-enable products from pill bottles to plant waterers, you can be sure of only one thing: the biggest IoT has yet to be imagined. (...)

If the Commission approves my proposal next month, the United States will be the first country in the world to open up high-band spectrum for 5G networks and applications. And that's damn important because it means U.S. companies will be first out of the gate. (...)

Unlike some countries, we do not believe we should spend the next couple of years studying what 5G should be, how it should operate, and how to allocate spectrum, based on those assumptions.

Like the examples I gave earlier, the future has a way of inventing itself. Turning innovators loose is far preferable to expecting committees and regulators to define the future.

We won't wait for the standards to be first developed in the sometimes arduous standards-setting process or in a government-led activity. Instead, we will make ample spectrum available and then rely on a private sector-led process for producing technical standards best suited for those frequencies and use cases."

What this means, is that there will be no regulation on the biohazard impacts for human life and health. Everything goes in the advancement of technology. And many will die to feed this greed that will have no limits.

Is is then with no surprise that COVID-19 was launched at the exact same time, to hide the effects of 5G.

Despite the fact — stated by many doctors and scientists, such as Dr. Shiva Ayyuardi — that this virus is a bioweapon, it is also clear, by the data obtained, that it doesn't justify a worldwide quarantine.

So, why would this quarantine be enforced on the people?

"The coronavirus fear mongering by the Deep State will go down in history as one of the biggest fraud to manipulate economies, suppress dissent and push mandated medicine" (Dr. Shiva Ayyadurai, MIT PhD, and expert in Biological Engineering).

Chapter 16: Hell on Earth.

How far can the greed of the elite go?

Tom Wheeler said it in his public the speech of June 2016:

"The main value of 5G will not be found in workshare or intellectual property. The main value of 5G by far will be in consumption rather than production. It will be in material gains and improvements in quality of life and economic opportunity."

This is the end of capitalism and the birth of worldwide communism. Because if there is no value in the intellectual property, this means the end of business as we know it.

He also states that there will be no value on the workshare either. The value is in the "consumption rather than production".

In other words, human life will become obsolete, because most employees won't be necessary anymore.

The quality of life will then necessarily continue through Artificial Intelligence and a collective grid, which he describes as "the cloud".

This universal network makes evolution a process at the hands of a few and for the collective good. This collective, according to him, will be merely composed by consumers. But what can people consume if they have no money to pay?

This is where Microsoft patent 666 comes to the picture. It involves inserting microchips into people's body to mine their activity for cryptocurrency purposes.

Basically, the sector of the population that survives the 5G radiation massacre, pollution, mass starvation, increase on crime rates all over the globe and mass unemployment, in a economic depression never before seen in our history, will be paid for a multitude of services, which don't necessarily include productivity.

Some people, will be used for research purposes and marketing, others for entertainment purposes, and sexual gratification, including prostitution, as we see today through social media, and some others will actually feed the elite, not only through thoughts and ideas but a lot much more.

The legal document within the section "Detailed Description of Embodiments, article 36, goes in detail of what type of body activity Microsoft intends to track:

"The body activity may include, for example, but not limited to, radiation emitted from human body, brain activities, body fluid flow (e.g. blood flow), organ activity or movement, body movement, and any other activities that can be sensed and represented by images, waves, signals, texts, numbers, degrees, or any other form of information or data. Examples of body radiation emitted from human body may include radiant heat of the body, pulse rate, or brain wave. Brain waves may comprise, for example, but not limited to, (i) gamma waves, involved in learning or memory tasks, (ii) beta waves, involved in logical thinking and/or conscious thought, (iii) alpha waves, which may be related to subconscious thoughts, (iv) theta waves, which may be related to thoughts involving deep and raw emotions, (v) delta waves, which may be involved in sleep or deep relaxation, or (vi) electroencephalogram (EEG), which may be measurement used to evaluate the electrical activity in the brain, such as deep concentration. Examples of the body movement may include eye movement, facial movement or any other muscular movements. Furthermore, brain activity can be sensed using the fMRI. The fMRI measures brain activity by detecting changes associated with blood flow. This technique relies on the fact that cerebral blood flow and neuronal activation are coupled. When an area of the brain is in use, blood flow to that region also increases."

This means a dictatorship at a very physical and even spiritual level.

If Microsoft can then pay you for learning something they decide to be beneficial for the collective, or for performing a certain behavior and reward you with cryptocurrency similar to Bitcoin, they can also punish you for unapproved subconscious thoughts or interactions, ban you for thinking the wrong thoughts, and even arrested you on the basis of pre-crime. That is, thinking about an illegal activity that you haven't done yet.

The merging of currency through biometric data with your thoughts, combined with ID2020, means that any thought against the system can penalize you severely and may also mean starving yourself to death.

You will simply not have the freedom to think any longer.

Another purpose of Microsoft's ID2020 is the use of its system for imposing vaccine compliance, meaning that the population will be forced to take a vaccine, that will contain chemicals and DNA, that will make it docile and obedience enough, but also corrupt its own evolution as a species.

This means having a DNA evolution for the elite, and another for the masses. In other words, they will separate human evolution in two different specimens:

One will be you — the retarded and animal-like humans;

and another will be them — the super intelligent and cybernetic god-like humans, harvesting from the cloud, which will be fed with their slaves' thoughts.

Now, who will control all these thoughts?

Surely, a human can't process so much information. But AI can. Humanity will be monitored and controlled through a computer.

God will be replaced by AI, and no human on earth will eat or even think, outside that monitoring grid.

That is why this is hell on earth. There will be no more spirituality or any type of spiritual activity or thought whatsoever. It is, quite simply, the perfect utopia for the atheists, who are dominated and inspired by sadistic, psychopathic and devilish ideas.

This, my friend, is Satan's utopia.

Chapter 17: The Darkness of the Power Elite.

The self-proclaimed "Illuminati" exist only because the rest have willingly accepted the darkness of ignorance.

The Rockefeller Foundation has controlled many institutions and universities to ensure that the majority remains stupid. And all of psychology and psychiatry, in fact, are fields of knowledge that have everything to do with mass control, and nothing to do with mental health.

This was something I realized a long time ago, and that even my colleagues from psychology admitted. But of course, people want a job, and then they end up being silent, if they don't want to lose their own career or certificate.

This is the same case with the police, the doctors, the scientists, and so on. To risk exposing the Elite is to risk losing an entire career and a future too. It is to risk being unemployed for a very long time, and wasting an entire life experience.

I also know that there are many, so called, "Illuminati parties" where there are orgies and many macabre things going on, like drinking human blood. But this has nothing to do with religion or spirituality.

To understand these people and their behaviors you have to read about psychopathy. That is where everything starts to make sense, even far before we enter the realm of demonic possession.

Aleister Crowley, whom they worship, actually ends up describing the level of stupidity of such people, because Crowley, despite his many attempts, was not even able to properly write a good manifesto on demonology.

For a person who proclaimed himself to the beast, he ended up looking more like an angry gremlin.

When people have no religion, they become obsessed with the subject of physical immortality and sexuality. It's a natural and predictable tendency of the human mind. Reason why believing in a God automatically redirects one towards mental health and a better channeling of our chakras' energy.

That is also why such people drink blood. They believe that blood helps in renewing the body. And they are right. The Aztecs, the Indians and the Chinese, among other cultures in history believe the same.

In fact, the Chinese torture animals before murdering them because they believe that the chemicals released during the state of fear increase the potential energy of the blood and meat consumed.

This said, yes, in a group of psychopaths, anything goes to promote eternal life. But a lot of these people come from different groups of society and religion. And there are those who believe that many Catholic priests are involved in this as well.

Moreover, the Vatican has already been exposed by many exorcists as the real home of the devil. It is, at very least, the home of a huge group of homosexuals and pedophiles.

In some of the most controversial interviews ever given, whistleblowers said the most horrific blood rituals occur in hidden chambers of Vatican. But we can only speculate about it, since the Vatican keeps itself locked and surrounded by big walls.

We cannot deny, nonetheless, that whenever a new Pope seemed to oppose the Jesuits, he appeared mysteriously dead just weeks later after assuming power, as was the case of Pope John Paul I. Which means the Pope of the Catholic Church is merely a symbol and not the true power behind the Catholic Church.

In short, those who are in the highest positions of power, are atheists, psychopaths, technocrats and bureaucrats, who control the world through vast amounts of wealths and powerful business corporations.

Bill Gates and his messianic complex is an example of this.

He believes that he is on earth to save the planet, by killing the majority in order to create a utopia for the survivors. And with such assumption, he ends up becoming one of the most famous psychopaths in history.

He also managed to get the entire planet depending on computers, so it's normal for him to have this distorted view of himself. As mentioned before, they are atheists, and atheists only see themselves as the objective of their own existence.

Many christians and muslims claim that he is not the antichrist because they cling too much to their own holy books, which the Power Elite has been using to facilitate their own plans.

Perhaps, from the point of view of the Bible or the Quran, Bill Gates is not the antichrist, but from the point of view of Bill Gates, himself, he definitely is and wants to be.

Bill Gates does everything as if he was a prophet and a visionary. And yet, he ends up becoming a criminal of the highest order. And the most amazing thing in all this, is that he is everywhere, and no one realizes the obvious: A liar so famous, that nobody realizes what a liar he is.

Chapter 18: How is the Mass Deception Kept Hidden?

To say that Bill Gates, the Rockefeller Family and the others associates of their plans, such as the Clintons and the Rothschilds, are the Illuminati, is absurd. But that's how they wish to be seen, as a superior and enlightened Elite.

Whenever the masses label them as the Illuminati, the masses are unknowingly giving them such authority and power. It's a form of respect to believe that.

They are not the Illuminati! They symbolize darkness of the most profound order. They are pure evil and symbolize a total lack of consciousness and the dangers of power, wealth and intelligence when associated with atheism. In other words, they are horribly sick and disgusting.

Their only source of power comes as a counter-balance to an extremely ignorant majority.

"In the big lie there is always a certain force of credibility; because the broad masses, in the primitive simplicity of their minds, more readily fall victims to the big lie than the small lie, since they themselves often tell small lies in little matters but would be ashamed to resort to large-scale falsehoods. It would never come into their heads to fabricate colossal untruths, and they would not believe that others could have the impudence to distort the truth so infamously. Even though the facts which prove this to be so may be brought clearly to their minds, they will still doubt and waver and will continue to think that there may be some other explanation (Adolf Hitler, In Mein Kampf).

The real Illuminati are not known. They have always operated in the shadows.

As a matter of fact, the real Illuminati are the ones systematically destroying the plans of these Elites — which have always emerged throughout history as a representation of human ignorance and evilness at the highest level of use — and by promoting a brighter future to the masses.

The masses are, and have always been, nothing more than victims of their own ignorance, delusions, laziness and stupid acts.

That is why these same masses have always been deceived, through their own revolutions, to promote the saviors who would then become their dictators, namely, with the French Revolution and the Russian Revolution.

The masses are stupid and that's why they are easily deceived. However, they have always insulted and murdered their own and true saviors.

We could therefore say that people deserve what they get. Or as Jesus said, "my people are destroyed because they are ignorant" (Hosea 4:6).

Despite knowing this, the real Illuminati are not asleep and are ready to give their life to change any outcome. And they will. Because the true Illuminati are blessed by the Light of God.

They will always find a way to change everything because this planet does not belong to a class of atheists.

Such individuals are the ones to call upon the power of God and manifest miracles beyond human predictability or comprehension.

This spiritual war, however, is made difficult because it is hard to fight an army of nearly eight billion zombies, willing to protect their masters under the influence of fear.

The odds are not and never in favor of the true enlightened ones.

The real Illuminati are very few and not the ones who control the world through wealth and coercion. But they are indeed the ones who can change everything with what could be called Divine Magick.

It is believed that some of them may be behind movements such as the New Age Movement, as a way of changing future events by releasing partial knowledge about magick to the masses.

Unfortunately, these masses are too dumb and selfish to understand the value of such gifts, and ended up focusing almost exclusively on using such previously hidden knowledge to acquire financial wealth and sex only.

The majority wastes very valuable information because their spiritual level is too low to comprehend the vastness of the power they misuse.

These masses are more focused on allegories and metaphors than the truth itself. And they can't perceive happiness beyond physical and personal acquisitions.

Chapter 19: The History of the Big Illusion.

Whoever says Freemasons control the world has clearly no idea of what he is saying, and is extremely, really far, from understanding anything about how this world is controlled.

It is a tendency of the human mind to simplify everything. That is why our history books are full of garbage. Or, as some would say: If the news are fake, imagine how fake is our entire history!

Although the Freemasons and their legends of a connection to the Knights Templar, along with a fairytale about secret magic scrolls found in Jerusalem in the middle ages, is the common assumption for the lineage and history of the Power Elite, it's actually just the story that most can perceive from their lack of ability to truly understand beyond that and due to the limitations imposed from above.

The true story, like the history of mankind, and also every man on Earth, is much more complex than it seems, or would be desirable to know, in order to explain it well or even to be accepted.

Our world has achieved such a level of deception, that most will either angrily, or laughably, reject the true facts at this point, even if shown with the necessary evidence.

As an example, the scrolls of Nag Hammadi, although being enough to discredit the whole Christian faith as it is known today, received a reaction that proves how much humanity doesn't care about the truth, but instead prefers neurotic fairytales invented within their social circles, and that are more easily accepted by their level of conscience.

This is the real reason why the Power Elite continues on increasing their wealth and power over the masses while restricting their own freedom.

This has nothing to do with secret societies or religious orders but the greed that our human nature, when detached from moral values, tends to make prevail in our actions.

This greed is empowered by knowledge, but we shouldn't be burning books or reject such knowledge, as what happened during the Inquisition and World War 2. We should instead share it and learn it, while using it to choose more positive individuals for leadership roles, as it was intended by those that kept it a secret in the beginning of times. Namely, the Pythagorean Brotherhood, from which most of the European Secret Societies emerge.

The intention of these first societies to stay secret, was related to the need of selecting only the noblest hearts to share the mystical wisdom. People who possessed the value and integrity that made the foundation for the application of the highest knowledge to the common good.

Over the years, this secrecy allowed that many powerful, rich and influential individuals of evil nature, namely, from a corrupt aristocracy, could access a tremendous amount of information that allowed them to go far beyond what they would have done without it.

There is indeed nothing in common between the virtuous ones that kept this wisdom a secret in order to protect it from falling into the wrong hands and those who keep it now secret to empower their own families and secure their wealth for future generations.

As an analogy, we can compare the Christians that beat their wives and children after a Sunday mass with the rest. Or the cult leaders that take the life of their followers, with those who uplift them and are still worshiped and followed far after their death.

Just like we can't say that all priests are pedophiles because of the acts of some, we can't say that all secret societies are dangerous as well.

Only a mad man wouldn't see the difference and only an ignorant man wouldn't consider the similarities.

As a matter of fact, and as I have personally witnessed many times, the real problem with all religions, from the bottom to the top, from the most open and naive, to the most abstract and elitist, is always the same: A misinterpretation of their own scriptures, a lack of ethics and a narcissistic viewpoint that contradicts the noblest human values, such as compassion, honesty, kindness and mercy.

What I wish to say here is that, it is the cruelty, greed and ignorance of men that we must fear, and not the wisdom they misuse, and certainly not the wise that possess it.

Chapter 20: The Portal to the Truth.

The portal to the truth is the human mind, when we connect the heart with the pineal gland — the center of our spiritual senses.

There are many ways to reach this center, namely, through different forms of meditation that imply exteriorizing our emotions. But the effect is better absorbed when the mind already contains enough synapses to process what is new. And there is only one day to accomplish this: through reading about the truth.

This is why you must know what to learn before learning anything.

In fact, and for the past years since this book was published, it has saved many lives that the world needs, uplifting it with information that is among us since the beginning of human history.

It has also saved the lives of individuals who, without it, would be lost and vulnerable to a predatory world that rejects them for seeing more, acknowledging faster and being kinder than the animalistic majority.

The knowledge that I expose here has saved my life countless times as well, and mainly when I needed it the most. Even though, having seen the arrogance and selfishness of this world, I cannot say that I'm writing these pages for the love of it, or for the love of the human race. And I certainly understand why it had to be kept a secret for thousands of years.

I'm writing this book for those that, like me, need it and will always, one way or another, find it, because that's their destiny, and God wouldn't want it otherwise, to fulfill His goals of having a prosperous and positively vibrant society, instead of the one that we have become accustomed to accept and that we can't possibly assimilate as being normal.

While the world tries to quickly erase, from the collective memory and its books, the acts of evil, destruction and crime, perpetrated by human beings against one another, acts that have always certainly been more prominent among the weak than in the strongest, it is said that a few special ones have saved mankind, with their wisdom, art, intentions and books. And "we know that even today only a very small percentage are ready to live as near the truth as they see it, to confess it and profess it before men by service and by righteous and harmless living" (Max Heindel, Rosicrucian Fellowship).

It must be clearly stated that they had the knowledge presented in these pages, and therefore it must continue being shared, otherwise there's no salvation possible for anyone. For as "man has gotten up to the potential of destroying the planet, he must now be pushed on up to the capability and actions of saving it" (Ron Hubbard, Founder of Scientology).

This ancient wisdom is the true reason why Christ and many other masters of these spiritual insights were murdered and their knowledge corrupted afterwards by men of greed and lust for power. And it has always occurred with the support of the masses and the silence of those with a good heart, the ones who could see it, but were too afraid to interfere.

"All that is necessary for the triumph of evil is that good men do nothing" (Edmund Burke, Freemason), but "silence in the face of evil is itself evil: God will not hold us guiltless. Not to speak is to speak. Not to act is to act (Dietrich Bonhoeffer, Founder of the Confessing Church and murdered in a concentration camp).

"Those who make peaceful revolution impossible, make violent revolution inevitable (John F. Kennedy, member of the Knights of Columbus and murdered for being opposed to secrecy).

Men shouldn't fear or hate what they do not know but study it and share it instead. For it is both an act of selfishness and cruelty to seek for the destruction of wisdom and the wise, but also to keep silent when witnessing it happening.

This said, let us learn about it and share it with others that can use it wisely and for a good end. For such is the kindest and most loving attitude anyone can have for mankind to survive and understand its purpose on earth and inside the cosmos of other interplanetary families.

Chapter 21: The Truth Uniting All Faiths.

If the members of every religion and secret society in the world truly knew the source of their belief system, they wouldn't follow their priests, leaders and prophets, but would instead search for the immediate link within that lineage. Because all religious dogmas seem separated, when in fact they're united under the same rules and divided only by interpretations and groups.

The holy scriptures of Hinduism, for example, don't actually belong to Hinduism. Hinduism and Sikhism are just organized religions that took them and used them, further enriching this compilation of texts with others written by the leaders of these groups.

Let us not forget that, in ancient times, there were no copyrights, and so it was easy to create a multitude of groups that copied the same texts and then translated them in their own way, from which the bible is merely one example.

The bible is a specific compilation of selected texts that were translated in ways that actually drastically change and corrupt the source from which they were taken.

In order to make this compilation credible to the masses, a huge amount of ancient gnostic texts written by the apostles were refused and then destroyed. The followers of such texts were then persecuted. And the Inquisition is one of the most visible examples of such persecution. Even though it had started far before, when the Christian Roman Empire was avoiding religious competition from other opposing systems of belief.

This situation continued until later years, with the persecution of the Protestant Church in Europe.

Today, there's a huge amount of information available, which can make religious people look dumb. But, if you start a religion, you can't use that information, because it has copyright ownership, and that's the irony of the modern world.

One thousand years ago, a book like this one would be seen by some as heretic and others as amazing. The firsts would try to destroy it and silence its author, while the seconds, a wise, bright, curious and enlightened minority, would try to protect it and create a society around it to share it.

This book could easily become the foundation of a new secret society, but in today's world, it is simply one more among millions, and sharing the same truth in a different viewpoint, just like other books about spirituality.

What differentiates this from many other books are the qualities that the author embodies it with: pragmatism and a type of honesty possible only through direct experience with these topics and a willingness to share the truth under the light of a complete faith in God.

Chapter 22: How to Investigate the Truth?

If we want to understand the delusional source of the material world, from which all misunderstandings arise, the acknowledgement of what I just said is a good starting point.

God, however, has a way of forcing evolution on a stubborn majority. This occurs through frequencies that cross the cosmos and enter our realm.

When stagnation appears and spreads, a few will break free, and become the rebels that push humanity forward and into that light.

These rebels that I am referring to, are the true illuminati, the ones that have always appeared in the shadows to create significant transitions in the world, even if at the cost of their own life.

One of such examples appeared with the medieval Order of the Knights Templar.

This order is indeed responsible for the Power Elite of our modern world, but they were already part of it in the medieval period, as the order was interconnected with the European nobility.

They also infiltrated the nobility in order to change it from the inside, which resulted in the many problems they later faced, namely, with the King of France — King Philip IV.

In what regards their knowledge, it has many roots, as the members of this society had a huge curiosity for the truth about Jesus Christ. As mentioned, the noble class was part of the group, and had its own interest on the topic as well.

Eventually, the evidence they found about Christ opposed what they had been taught by the Roman Church, the most powerful organization in Europe after the fall of the Roman Empire. This knowledge wasn't complete and had many influences, but allowed a better understanding of ancient mysteries, which these knights dedicated themselves to study.

They would later become one of the sources spreading what today is known as alchemy — a mixture of esoteric knowledge from the middle east combined with the occult teachings of christ.

In order to resume a complex story in a few words, that couldn't possibly be enough to clarify well-known concepts, let us just say that Jesus wasn't a carpenter but a builder, and that is from where the words alchemist and mason originate.

Jesus was teaching Gnosticism to his followers, which consists of the art of empowering the spirit through the art of transmutation, in order to understand and change reality with the power of thought and faith.

Today, followers of the New Age Movement would call it the Law of Attraction, the Law of Vibration, or Magick, which, ironically, is opposed by many modern Christians.

This school of knowledge was passed unto him by other traditions found in those locations, and it is based on the same principles to be found in the ancient Indian, Tibetan, Sumerian, Babylonian, Egyptian, Persian, Greek and even the lost Atlantic traditions.

Even the many modern translations of the Bible contain the same knowledge, although written in code, which allows secret societies to study the same book from a perspective unknown and even preposterous to mainstream Christians.

These codes are present at many levels. The blind will see none but the metaphorical aspect presented. But those who are enlightened can go deeper and find many metaphysical representations within the same lines.

Enlightenment, according to these traditions, consists of the unlimited but cyclic process of investigating the many layers of the truth, even if it implies reviewing the same literature multiple times.

Chapter 23: The Secret Within Humanity.

With this secret knowledge in their hands, the Knights were able to accumulate great power and wealth in a short period of time, making themselves threatening to the kings of Europe and the Roman Church.

Their true religion became one beneath another — christians to the outsiders but gnostics to the insiders.

The Templars were the ones who brought to Europe real Christianity, which matches many other philosophical approaches, and were also the first society in Europe to create a banking system, having Switzerland as their headquarters.

Despite this and what many may say against them, the Templars contributed to the expansion of Christianity, by directly sponsoring the construction of numerous churches, all of which possess their symbols, understood today as logos, such as the templar cross.

When accused of heresy and persecuted, they had to disappear from the public eye, but were able to keep their power and influence by rewriting history in a way that is gradually becoming exposed in our days, in this era of awakening, the Era of Aquarius.

For this reason, I must say that, even though the Freemasons claim to descend from the Knights Templar, as in other religions, the truth is more complex, and this isn't necessarily true, despite the fact that we can't deny, at the very least, an indirect lineage.

This same indirect lineage is the one that many other orders, claiming today to be descendants from these Knights Templar, also have.

The complexity and the mystery surrounding the templars is still too vast for most people to comprehend, and by far extends beyond their military purpose.

The Knights Templar learned many mystical philosophies from the ancient Sumerian, Mesopotamian, Egyptian, Essene and Gnostic priesthoods.

How is that possible?

Well, in those times, there wasn't such homogeneity among people as we see today, or a strong monotheism in religious practices, so it was a lot easier to find followers of different beliefs and many texts that hadn't yet been destroyed by the ignorance of men.

Diversity was actually far more prominent than what we see today.

Even Pompei had specific streets for religious practice, where the population would gather and then divide themselves in the direction of different temples, according to their faith. And isn't it ironic that religious tolerance was more common before than it is now?

We wish to see history in a linear form, but history itself is complex and doesn't obey our desires. It is composed by cycles and these cycles don't follow the same rhythms.

Besides that, at the time of the crusades, there were many and different secret mystic schools in the Middle East directly linked to the Greek mystic schools followed by Plato, Socrates and Pythagoras, which had taken knowledge obtained from the Egyptian schools, reason why Plato knew about Atlantis.

Chapter 24: The Importance of a Religious Education.

The world has always been divided between people's religion and the elite's religion, so in fact many famous individuals in human history were educated in the ancient mysteries and esoteric arts, while the rest worshipped figures of stone and symbols.

What we can see in India today is an example of that ancient reality. For the poor and uneducated majority worship monsters and gods made of clay and stone, while wise individuals become extremely rich and powerful with the exact same ancient wisdom.

The wide division between the elites and the uneducated who follow the same scriptures occurs because the masses can't understand what they read and the elite doesn't want them to understand either.

If the masses made efforts to understand those writings in a way that defies their schizophrenic belief-system and the elite helped them become enlightened, then there wouldn't be any elite in the first place, and people couldn't be ruled.

As Osho (founder of the Rajneesh Movement) said, "No society wants you to become wise. It is against the investment of all societies.

If people are wise they cannot be exploited. If they are intelligent they cannot be subjugated, they cannot be forced into a mechanical life, to live like robots. They will assert themselves — they will assert their individuality. They will have the fragrance of rebellion around them; they will want to live in freedom.

Freedom comes with wisdom. Intrinsically, they are inseparable. And no society wants people to be free. The communist society, the fascist society, the capitalist society, the Hindu, the Mohammedan, the Christian — no society likes people to use their own intelligence. Because the moment they start using their intelligence, they become dangerous — dangerous to the establishment, dangerous to the people who are in power, dangerous to the "haves"; dangerous to all kinds of oppression, exploitation, suppression; dangerous to the churches, dangerous to the states, dangerous to the nations.

In fact, a wise man is afire, alive, aflame. He would like rather to die than to be enslaved. Death will not matter much to him.

He cannot sell his life to all kinds of stupidities, to all kinds of stupid people. He cannot serve them. Hence, the societies down the ages have been supplying you with false knowing. That's the very function of your schools, colleges, universities. They don't serve you.

Remember: they serve the past, they serve the vested interests.

Of course, they go on puffing your ego up to make it bigger and bigger; they go on giving you more and more degrees. Your name becomes longer and longer. But only the name; You go on becoming shorter and shorter.

A point comes where there are only certificates and the man has disappeared.

First the man carries the certificates, then the certificates carry the man. The man is long dead."

It is for this reason that the greatest fear of the Elites has always been a well-educated anarchist majority.

Anarchism, in its purest form, as portrayed by societies like the Native Americans, is one of the most feared form of organizations. Reason why, after being pushed to concentration camps, the Native Americans continued suffering persecution in many different ways.

Their way of life and their culture is a threat to the establishment in which they live, a system which has put efforts to indoctrinate the younger generations in order to eradicate such values from them.

The opposite path would lead to the anarchy we were taught to fear, in which everyone would be fully responsible for his own life, and the moral standards of society would be so high that we wouldn't have to fear criminality, rivalry and jealousy anymore.

However, as long as we believe that we are just intellectual monkeys, subjugated by authority, and with no capacity to rule over ourselves and exercise discipline and honor without the surveillance of the police, with no spiritual capacity to elevate ourselves, that won't ever happen.

This is why monitor human thoughts, and in particular, through the use of ridicule and discrimination, as what people do to one another, is so important to keep the masses organized like sheep. Except that these masses keeps themselves in line themselves by moral codes that work against them and their best interests.

The idea that one has the right to judge someone based on his values and beliefs is the most dangerous and ridiculous of all, and has let to the absurdity of condemning those who speak based on research, as if their research was as valid as a dumb and personal opinion with not foundation.

We saw this with Dr. Jordan Peterson, a professor who clashed against mainstream beliefs (having no scientific basis) with his scientific background, proving that the masses are too brainwashed at this point to be able to see the obvious.

If anything, the attacks he received proved that the masses are well under control, as much as they were during the Bolshevik Revolution.

The problem is that the masses are unaware that they are being controlled through the use of liberalism, socialism and popularism, they won't be able to notice when their rights are taken away by authoritarianism. And by the time they do notice, it will be too late for them.

Chapter 25: Why Religion Always Degenerates.

It is a natural tendency of the human family of Earth to follow patterns related to greed and jealousy, as much as it is to degenerate and disintegrate itself. All societies followed the same cycle, by rising and falling, and then vanishing.

While some believe that this occurs due to outside forces, of a mystical nature, and others more pessimistic, believe humans in general are worthless creatures with no principles, I believe that this occurs because humanity as a collective, has not evolved up to a state in which it can appreciate itself and survive as such.

It is because the spiritual condition on earth is so low, that humans keep self-destroying.

This hypothesis can easily be proven when we compare different cultures, and then place them between their values and their sociocultural problems.

For example, Lithuania is a country where the locals are known for being the most xenophobic and racist in all of Europe. They are also proud to be atheists. And then you look at their social interactions and you verify that they are all ruled by an anxiety for validation.

Why? Because the more you remove God from a culture, the more the people will seek for approval among themselves. Their moral becomes the moral of the group.

However, if this group has no moral in itself, and hates any interference from the outside, you create a kind of entropy, in which the members of the society feel detached from everyone and eventually themselves too. Depression follows and then suicide as well.

This is why Lithuania, despite being a tiny country on the map, leads the world in the number of suicides per capita.

It's actually ironic, how a civilization fears the outside so much that it ends self-destroying itself from the inside.

On the other hand, what chance do these people have, when they insult people like me? If they insult those who know more than them, they can only be proud to be stupid. And that's what I saw in this nation: the most stupid and arrogant of dozens of many other nations I visited, justifying the fact that some countries and cultures contribute more for the planet when disappearing from history.

Now, you analyze this dynamic from the religious point of view, and you will see that all religions, due to the fact that they are composed of individuals attached to a system that indoctrinates them on the wrong values, are doomed to fail as well.

In fact, a great part of the work that a religious scholar must go through, is related first and foremost towards himself, towards the detaching from the wrong values, detaching from self-pity and detaching from jealousy.

"Wisdom needs a totally different approach, a diametrically opposite approach. Knowledge is of the mind, wisdom is a state of no-mind" (Osho, founder of Rajneesh). And until one understand this, he is a threat to his own group, no matter how many decades have past.

This is why I was able to correct members from different secret societies in regards to information that they had wrongly assimilated for decades. They did that because the ego is obsessed with its own self-reflection.

People always seek validation through comfort, rather than the destruction of that which causes the need — a lack of identification with a decadent society.

The story of Jesus follows the exact same pattern. Christians started worshiping symbols and a God, a ruler of gods, while in fact Jesus was a gnostic, and Gnosticism is a completely different philosophy, also related to Hinduism and Buddhism.

There is actually evidence and many documents proving that he was in India and Tibet, even in the Bible. Because Jesus was unknown until he was 30 years old. Before that, the Bible merely says that he had disappeared for several years of his life, while the Tibetans have evidence showing that he was there during this period studying their own texts.

Chapter 26: The Legacy of Jesus.

In what concerns the legacy of Jesus, to the Gnostics Mary Magdalene was the person to whom Jesus entrusted his church. But the other apostles envied her, so she was eventually slandered by Christianity.

Peter, the first Pope, told Jesus: "Make Mary leave us, for females don't deserve life" (Gospel of Thomas), "we are not able to suffer this woman who takes the opportunity from us" (In The Pistis Sophia).

In regards to this situation, Mary, with a premonitory care and a tremendous demonstration of empathy, later warns Jesus: "I am afraid of Peter, for he threatens me and hates our race (the Gnostics)" (In The Pistis Sophia).

The apostles disliked her because she was "the knower, the one who understands, the one who is sensual and wise, sensitive and emotional" (Jane Schaberg, Professor of Religious Studies at the University of Detroit Mercy).

Mainstream Christianity describes Mary Magdalene as a penitent sinner and a redeemed prostitute, but in Gnosticism she's seen as the true leader of the Christian Church.

Why was she the true leader? Because Jesus "loved her more than the other disciples" (In The Gospel of Philip) and "more than the rest of the women" (In The Gospel of Mary), and said to her, "Mary, thou blessed one, who I will complete in all the mysteries" (The Pistis Sophia), because "I have given you authority over all things and Sons of Light" (The Sophia of Jesus Christ).

Despite the hatred and jealousy among the apostles, Mary never lost hope on them. After comforting the Apostles because of the departure of Christ, Mary Magdalene tells them: "What is hidden from you, I will proclaim to you" (The Gospel of Mary).

That, however, would never occur.

During the time in which the apostles were being persecuted, she had to run away to the south of France, where legends about the first secret societies and Gnosticism started being spread in Europe.

According to the Knights Templar heirs of The Sovereign Magistral Order of the Temple of Solomon, "The heretical Gnostic story, which was passionately believed by the Templars, was that Jesus and Mary Magdalene had a daughter, named Sarah, and that with the help of Joseph of Arimathea, Jesus sent Mary on a boat through the Mediterranean Sea to arrive in the South of France, to begin a new life in safety with her daughter Sarah, and to begin teaching and spreading the Gospels as one of the Apostles".

France is also the birthplace of the Knights Templar. And so, for all these reasons, France is seen by the Gnostics as the birthplace of European Gnosticism. And it is not a coincidence that the statue of liberty, in the USA, a gift from French freemasons, represents a pregnant woman with the torch of enlightenment in her hand.

It is also in France that Leonardo Da Vinci, author of the famous painting of the last supper of Christ, spent his last days and many other famous, and controversial artists, found shelter during a time in which their art and wisdom couldn't be freely expressed in Italy or other parts of Europe.

The painting of the last supper is an obvious evidence of the fact that Leonardo Da Vinci was a follower of Gnosticism, as he portrays Mary Magdalene as the wife of Christ and successor to his Church, but shows Peter holding a knife with his right hand, while threatening Mary Magdalene with the left hand to her throat, as if he was showing his intention of decapitating the head of true Christianity.

The use of sacred geometry in this painting, in parallel with the many layers of hidden truths that researchers are still uncovering to this day, is an evidence that he was a Rosicrucian as well.

Chapter 27: The Greatest Secrets Never Told.

Leonardo Da Vinci was a student of Gnosticism, Rosicrucian and Hermeticism — one of the real descendants of the Pythagorean Brotherhood.

His obsession with geometry and numerology — formerly known, when combined inside secret societies, as the book of nature — in alignment with spiritual symbolisms, shows us exactly that.

His immense wisdom was obtained directly from a lineage brought by the Knights Templar and other secret orders, and for this reason, was extremely focused on the common misinterpretation of Christianity. Something which, at that time, meant being accused of heresy and face the death penalty.

Da Vinci constantly challenged catholicism as a paid artist, and he did so elegantly, using the same techniques learned in his secret meetings.

His ability to challenge the prevailing powers with wisdom and the discernment of a secret agent, is eloquently explained in his differentiation between light and shadow, meaning enlightenment and darkness, or, the enlightened ones — The Illuminati — and those who are ignorant, and therefore living in the darkness, in the shadows of reality.

He said: "The beginnings and ends of a shadow are found between light and darkness and can be infinitely diminished as well as infinitely increased.

The shadow is then the means by which the bodies display themselves. The characteristics of these bodies could not be understood in detail without their shadows" (Leonardo da Vinci).

In other words, consciousness, is a transitory process between darkness and light, but it is in the manifestation of this dynamic that you understand the difference between the two states.

One can opt to turn more towards the light, or towards the darkness. But, in every step of our existence, our decisions determine our spiritual nature.

In explaining reality in such a way, he was addressing also the importance of qualities such as differentiation, analysis, compassion, empathy, responsibility and patience. And he was also saying that not all men are equal, for some have presented actions that position them closer to the light, while others have positioned themselves closer to the darkness.

This type of insights on reality emerged from an understanding of the alchemical transmutation of our soul towards the light — the God-like state for the Gnostics —, an inner process, related to self-reflection, and naturally, separated from the hierarchical order imposed by the Catholic Church.

This is why many Rosicrucians, in a humorous approach to themselves, tend to represent their temple as being a mirror with two candle next to it.

In truth, they meditate and pray by analyzing their own actions in relation to others, for they believe that everyone we encounter reflects an aspect of our inner nature, even and especially, when such person infuriates us.

A they say, "you cannot be infuriated by someone unless you possess within yourself the state that allows that to happen".

This doesn't mean that one must suppress his emotions, but rather understand such emotions as a reflection of something caused by the outside. For anger as a response to an insult, even when justified, emerges from an ego trying to protect itself. And what is an ego, but an illusion, when we look at ourselves as an eternal soul.

The same occurs when we are afraid, for fear reflects a lack of faith within us. And a lack of faith comes from lack of responsibility in creating and determining our own future.

The ideal state for a Rosicrucian is then that of no ego and no fear — a constant surveillance on one's emotions and a hawk-eye in the future.

That hawk-eye is the eye of Horus — always vigilant and always faithful to the plans of the Almighty God.

Chapter 28: Angels and Demons.

Obviously, these secret societies were kept secret to protect the knowledge from being found and destroyed, but also to protect the name and life of their members for the reasons already mentioned.

In time, the secrecy contributed to hide a vast influence of the future members of these orders in many historical events, even though, unfortunately, most of them with negative, megalomaniacal and revengeful repercussions over mankind.

The, so called, enlightened ones, would cast a shadow on the entire planet and attempt to control the darkness by themselves. And in doing so, they became immersed in such darkness, as the princes and princesses of Satan — The Satanic Monarchy.

A new army of enlightened ones, prepared to fight the corrupted Illuminati, would have to emerge from the masses and by the Divine will of God.

Some have referred to them as Indigo, Star Children, Wonderers, among many other names. All of which, are attempts at identifying them, in order to first discriminate them, and then destroy them. This way, they can't interfere with the, now extremely powerful, Elite.

Although most of these angels have lost themselves in many ways, were poisoned with psychiatric drugs and labeled as insane, or were murdered, or, as was often the case too, committed suicide, such army of "warrior angels" is still very active today, and in a human form.

It is very easy to identify them, as much as it is easy to identify those who are demonically possessed. Because both reflect the polarities that are at war against each other.

On one side of the battle, you find the Narcissists and Psychopaths;

On the other side, you find the Empaths and Spiritualists.

On the surface, however, they can be confused between each other. For many religious leaders, many famous speakers on spirituality and self-development, many doctors and scientists, and in general, many people who seem to want the common good, want to actually destroy humanity.

The only way to see this difference, without any doubt, comes in the form of their frequency. Their energies are completely different and emerge at different levels.

A demon always shows a specific frequency, of a lower nature. And can't be seen by their words, because they can manipulate crowds with much ease.

I know this because I have seen it. I can read their mind. And that is what makes me dangerous to such individuals. They know I can read their mind. And if you can read the mind of a demonically possessed individual, you can't be controlled. In fact, you are able to identify the thoughts of anyone on the planet and know their intentions too.

Mind reading is one of the capacities of those who are sent here by God. Premonition is another. Humans can't do this. Only demons can. But although both angels and demons are gifted with the same spiritual powers, they cannot share the same space without knowing that they are enemies.

The energy between the who forces are too different, for one group represents darkness and another the light.

When both confront each other, people observe them in complete ignorance, because the common human, is too stupid to see the difference between good and evil.

However, I have just told you how to analyze it. Evil, demonic possession, psychopathy and narcissism, are all characteristics of the same darkness, and can be effectively described through these different approaches, and match in every description.

In other words, there is no difference between those four manifestations and there is no point in differentiating them either.

Also by Dan Desmarques

Spiritual Warfare: What You Need to Know About Overcoming Adversity

Collective Consciousness: How to Transcend Mass Consciousness and Become One With the Universe

The Spiritual Mechanics of Love: Secrets They Don't Want You to Know about Understanding and Processing Emotions

The 10 Laws of Transmutation: The Multidimensional Power of Your Subconscious Mind

The Evil Within: The Spiritual Battle in Your Mind

Deception: When Everything You Know about God is Wrong

How to Change the World: The Path of Global Ascension Through Consciousness

Religious Leadership: The 8 Rules Behind Successful Congregations

The 14 Karmic Laws of Love: How to Develop a Healthy and Conscious Relationship With Your Soulmate

A New Way of Being: How to Rewire Your Brain and Take Control of Your Life

Uma Nova Forma de Existir: Como Organizar Sua Mente e Assumir o Controle da Sua Vida

O Propósito da Sua Alma: A Reencarnação e o Espectro da Consciência na Evolução

Your Soul Purpose: Reincarnation and the Spectrum of Consciousness in Human Evolution

Encontre Seu fluxo: Como Adquirir a Sabedoria e o Conhecimento de Deus

Find Your Flow: How to Get Wisdom and Knowledge from God

66 Days to Change Your Life: 12 Steps to Effortlessly Remove Mental Blocks, Reprogram Your Brain and Become a Money Magnet

66 Dias Para Mudar Sua Vida: 12 Etapas Para Remover Bloqueios Mentais, Reprogramar Seu Cérebro e Atrair Dinheiro

Consciência Coletiva: Como Transcender a Consciência de Massa e Se Tornar Um com o Universo

Batalha Espiritual: O Que Você Precisa Saber Para Superar a Adversidade

Codex Illuminatus: Quotes & Sayings of Dan Desmarques

Codex Illuminatus: Citações e Provérbios de Dan Desmarques

As 14 Leis Cármicas do Amor: Como Desenvolver Um Relacionamento Saudável e Consciente Com Sua Alma Gêmea

The Hidden Language of God: How to Find a Balance Between Freedom and Responsibility

Your Full Potential: How to Overcome Fear and Solve Any Problem

The Secret Science of the Soul: How to Transcend Common Sense and Get What You Really Want From Life

?????????????????????

Technocracy: The New World Order of the Illuminati and The Battle Between Good and Evil

About the Publisher

This book was published by 22Lions.com.
Follow us at Facebook.com/22lions